Cover photograph: The bell tower of Saint Andrew's Episcopal Church built in 1901 and located in Oregon Hill contrasts with the contemporary lines of the 26 story Federal Reserve Bank of Richmond.

Preceding photographs: Page 1, gas lamp and dogwood trees at dusk, the Fan District. Pages 2–3, monument to Hunter Holmes McGuire, grounds of the state capitol. Pages 4–5, Forest Hill Park, Southside. Pages 6–7, James Center Complex.

For additional information please consult the pictorial notes at the end of the book.

Book designer: Jeffrey B. Burt
Editorial Assistant: Susan Heroy
Photographs copyright © 1989 David R. White. All rights reserved
Text copyright © 1989 James S. Wamsley. All rights reserved
Library of Congress Catalog Number: 89-62037
First Edition

ISBN 1-882096-01-0
Printed and bound in Hong Kong
Published by: STOCKFILE, 1322 West Broad Street
P.O. Box 4902, Richmond, Va 23220
804-358-6364

Limited edition prints are available from this publication upon request.

STOCKFILE

RICHMOND

PORTRAIT OF A CITY

Photography By David R. White

Text By James S. Wamsley

Monument • Matthew Fontaine Maury

RICHMOND: A Personal Portrait

by James S. Wamsley

Lured by city lights and the jingle of $78 a week, I moved to Richmond
in the middle 1950s and signed on with the local bureau of The Associated
Press. The journey was an artistic success but a financial affliction. Even
then, more than 30 years ago, $78 provided the barest subsistence for a
young couple and their infant daughter. We relied heavily on macaroni
and cheese, relish sandwiches, and machine-shredded salad dispensed in
plastic bags by the Patterson Avenue A&P. It was a Spartan life, but we
were happy. I liked the wire service job and I liked Richmond, which
exuded a peculiar, absent-minded charm, elusively distant, rather like
native Richmonders themselves.

Here was an old city heavy with memories of triumph and calamity.
Along one hundred gritty streets—or so it seemed in my youthful
imagination—a dramatic past slumbered restively behind tall shuttered
windows, their gray paint dry and scaly as petrified bark. I liked making
solitary excursions through neighborhoods familiar to John Marshall,
Edgar Allan Poe, and Robert E. Lee. In the 1950s, some of those
partriarchal venues were, to put it charitably, in a state of decline. One of
them provided my favorite free parking place. When I drove downtown to
the AP bureau on Fourth Street, I headed first for the buckling streets and
sidewalks of nearby Gamble's Hill, a vicinity of inspired trashiness and
degradation.

Gamble's Hill, whose three-story townhouses once sheltered some of
Richmond's first families, fairly reeked of decayed gentility. Poe himself
might have conjured up Gamble's Hill as a setting for one of his
melancholy tales. At the hill's apogee or prow, jutting high above the
James River, an antebellum caprice called Pratt's Castle thrust up Gothic
Revival walls of simulated stone, black with age. Its forbidding gateways
and crenelated towers might have embosomed the owner of "The Tell-Tale
Heart," or even Vincent Price.

It is hard to understand fully how so convenient a neighborhood, so
distinguished once, so sited with wonderful views of the river, could have
got in such a fix. Doubtless the proximity of the Virginia State
Penitentiary on one side, and some ramshackle, superannuated industries
by the riverbank at its feet, were depressing factors. Yet in the midst of

this disintegration stood one wonderful old mansion on South Third Street where original, century-old standards prevailed. Dark and immaculate behind its cast-iron, granite-rooted fence, its brick and trim the brownish red of aged mahogany, the house was customarily shuttered tight against what Gamble's Hill had become. On rare moments around twilight, a partially-opened window disclosed a mid-Victorian parlor glowing in gentle refulgence, a room where General Lee might have called. The brassbound mail slot and mighty doorknob gleamed from years of polishing by, I suppose, the same hand that swabbed offending grime from the portico's black and white marble squares and reached out for the morning milk bottle that unfailingly waited, dewy and cool. But in at least six years of observing the place, I never saw a human being. It was said that the final occupant was a descendant of the first. One family, from start to finish. Like an outpost of culture enduring the Dark Ages, the old house defended its vanished world longer than any other. Even the graceful brick outhouse, built into the back garden wall, remained sturdy, and probably usable, until the day the bulldozer came.

Almost nothing remains today of what I have described.

Much of Gamble's Hill itself is gone, devoured by the Downtown Expressway. Beyond that canyon, overlooking the river where Pratt's Castle once stood, is the nouveau-Williamsburg headquarters complex of the Ethyl Corporation. Ethyl policed up the riverbank below, halted the deterioration of the ravaged Tredegar Iron Works, stabilized some interesting ruins, and reconstructed the historic cannon foundry of 1861. The scene around Gamble Hill's ample skirts is park-like today. Look eastward and the changes of thirty years are equally dramatic, with sparkling skyscrapers and landscaped plazas from Main Street to the James River, supplanting yesterday's seedy huddle of railroad sidings, warehouses, and ramshackle factories clinging to the riverside.

But the best view of all rewards those driving in from south of the river. The Manchester Bridge aims in a ramrod-straight, no-nonsense line at the fresh bright towers, then drops you off at their feet. The new Lee Bridge, a broad and graceful ramp in space, makes a more artful approach, displaying the city skyline asymmetrically on the right-hand side. Either way, the effect is breathtaking, and I cannot imagine being blasé about it. For those short inbound moments Richmond becomes the beckoning city of anyone's youthful dreams.

Changing almost imperceptively, one piece at a time, the cityscape—the big picture—has generally improved. Think of the old Ninth Street Bridge, a rickety, part wooden structure unsafe at any speed above a brisk crawl, now replaced by the Manchester Bridge with its graceful parabolic legs. A spindly eyesore called the Marshall Street Viaduct, after defacing Shockoe Valley for much of the century, was replaced by the monumental Martin Luther King Memorial Bridge. As for Richmond's most visible downtown thoroughfare, Broad Street, the picture is mixed. Around the Marriott Hotel, 6th Street Marketplace, and Richmond Centre there is obvious strength. A few blocks west, restorations in the Empire Theater area presage better times. Some other parts of Broad probably appeared smarter in the 1950s than today, but somehow, through all the tempests of change, Richmond's two great department stores, Miller & Rhoads and Thalhimers, have endured, immutable and comforting. Few other cities can make a comparable statement. Broad Street—endless as well as broad—stands today as a massive challenge and opportunity in the redevelopment of downtown.

In all, firmly bolted to what Edmund Spenser described as "the ever-whirling wheel of change," Virginia's capital has probably never looked better, yet I have mixed feelings about some of the side effects that the ever-whirling wheel spins off. I do not mourn the Edwardian warehouses removed to build new skyscrapers (when they are good skyscrapers) but other structures, like Pratt's Castle and the mysterious townhouse, were significant, oddly personal losses. They are tender spots in memory. When I am in another town and it becomes known that I hail from Richmond, someone always comments favorably on our rich history and our beautiful streets. "It's such a lovely old city," they say. We're known as a citadel of historic preservation. I find that reputation rich with irony because for so long it was underserved.

A former executive director of the Historic Richmond Foundation, which has labored for years to check the tide of demolition of significant structures, gave me an exceptionally subtle viewpoint. "The famous Virginia ancestor worship is in people's hearts, and does not require physical manifestations," said Michael W. Gold. "Places with less reverence for the past do more about preserving it."

Richmond had a big supply of old buildings, and many of them survived, not through care, but happenstance. When important buildings

were imperiled, some signal victories were won by dedicated amateurs, often considered difficult and even crackpotty by the majority. Other preservation successes have been engineered by non-natives.

A manufacturer from New York may have been the catalyst in beginning Richmond's downtown renaissance. Andrew J. Asch Jr. arrived in the 1950s, liked the city, and stayed. In the early 1960s a real estate agent took him to a rundown neighborhood called Shockoe Slip, and showed him a once-handsome commodities exchange building in its original 1871 state, crying out for help. Andy Asch bought it. Then he bought more buildings. A man who has described himself as an adaptive user, not a preservationist, Mr. Asch guided the redevelopment of Shockoe Slip along a tasteful middle road, toward equality and balance, not into the sort of "old town" entertainment center that bloomed and quickly faded in other cities. From the pioneer opening of Sam Miller's Exchange Cafe in 1973, "The Slip" has been a dynamo for downtown redevelopment, beneficial change, and preservation too.

In a way the neighborhood is holy ground. On May 27, 1607, only a week after arriving at Jamestown, an exploring party under Captain Christopher Newport arrived at the falls of the James, where on a small unrecorded island they set up a cross. After several false starts at a permanent settlement, a trading post took root in 1637. Presumably the English displaced the Indians who, perhaps for thousands of years, had conducted their own commerce from a large flat rock (Old Rock Landing, as the colonists called it) at the mouth of Shockoe Creek, or the foot of 17th Street today. The original William Byrd inherited the property in 1670. Richmond was known as Byrd's Warehouse—or Shocco—until after 1733, when William Byrd II grandly, and simultaneously, laid out the new cities of Richmond and Petersburg. The elegant, witty, secretly scandalous founding father described the sites as "naturally intended for Marts, where the Traffick of the Outer Inhabitants must center. Thus we did not build Castles only, but also Citys in the Air."

Recently I tried to find the site of the rock at Shockoe Creek and the river. It was hopeless; everything was paved over and built on; a sewage retaining basin may stand above the very site. As far as I could tell, Shockoe Creek does not exist. So much for the earliest landmark.

We might respect our predecessors more had they treated the city's very touchstone with more veneration, but let us not strain for too much

Preceding pages: Port of Richmond • James River

16

significance in one lapse of judgment. It is clear that early Richmonders regarded the river with respect and affection. Visitors and newcomers commented on the grandeur of the town's setting above the roaring rapids. The river was "raging with impetuosity, tumbling and dashing from rock to rock, with an astonishing roar," said an 18th century Englishman. Handsome houses on the summits of hills "commanded a wild, grand, and most elegant perspective." Visitors seemed struck by the noise of the falls, "a foaming uproar," which was borne by the wind for miles around.

Early drawings and paintings of Richmond invariably center on the spectacle of the James. Artists made focal points of proud engineering works like new railroad bridges towering on their stone pilings, and especially the James River and Kanawha Canal, gently curving past Hollywood Cemetery and around Gamble's Hill, a delightful prospect. I wish a first-rate painter—say George Caleb Bingham—had come through around 1855 and left us views of life around the canal basin. It must have been beautiful, that shimmering two-block-square lagoon between Cary and Canal Streets from 9th to 11th. With some imagination we can picture a colorful mingling of boatmen, merchants, and passengers conducting a daily pageant in the heart of the city. But after the 1870s, when the canal finally succumbed to the railroad, the basin was simply abandoned. Gradually and haphazardly it filled in and was overlaid with a railroad yard. I knew Richmonders who remembered the Great Basin still partially exposed as late as the 1920s.

From Main Street toward the river in the late 19th and early 20th centuries, the downtown scene grew ever more industrial, and ever less inviting, while retail and commercial development pushed west on Broad and Grace. Did Richmond turn its back on the James River? That was the effect, yet the movement only reflected the business dynamic of the times. Construction of the Jefferson Hotel in 1896 represented a massive vote of confidence in the westward commercial movement of Richmond. That confidence probably reached its peak with the city's major Art Deco landmark, the Central National Bank building. Begun in the 1920s, it was completed in 1930, just in time for the Great Depression. The *fin de siècle* streetscapes at its feet—scenes the artist Edward Hopper would have loved—remained undisturbed, preserved by hard times, while the bank stood like a monument to dimly remembered better days.

But when the better days returned, Richmond's important new buildings went elsewhere, beyond midtown Broad Street. The Reynolds Metals Company went to far-off West Broad in 1958 to build its new headquarters, a modern masterpiece almost temple-like in its purity, and infinitely more polished than the few other large structures of the Bauhaus era then being inflicted on Richmond. A few years later, when the first signs of a building revival appeared in the Main Street financial district, its expressions were mediocre at best. That was bad news because new construction between 7th and 14th Streets usually meant the destruction of entire rows of vintage classics, chiefly the noble, lamented ironfronts. We exchanged great buildings for commonplace ones, and further distanced ourselves—via chaotic individualism—from the handsome, unified 19th century city that Richmond once was. The local government provided little inspiration with a new city hall that managed to suggest both a mausoleum and an egg crate.

Major-league architecture returned downtown with Philip Johnson's design for WRVA Radio on Church Hill. Other strong hands produced the new Federal Reserve and Crestar buildings. Then came the entire cluster of the James Center, whitest of the bright towers so vivid from the southern approaches. Their construction produced a sensational brush

Still Life • Bateau artifacts

with the remote past, one that almost ended in fiasco. In August 1983, construction workers excavating for the first James Center buildings began digging into old boats buried more than 20 feet down. Several were hauled away and destroyed before the probing curiosity of amateur canal historians drew the admission from a construction worker that yes, some boats were down there.

A small army of more than 100 amateur diggers, hastily organized by the Archaeological Society of Virginia, plunged into the dirt as the contractor obligingly delayed the bulldozers. A fleet of boats remained, a treasury of information on the period of American canalling, which had been almost a total mystery. These boats, after decades of use, had sunk in the canal's turning basin, some long before the Civil War. I went down to look at them and found that each had a surviving personality. One of them went down—probably in the 1840s—with a cargo of coal, and the air around it reeked with the stench of damp sulphur. Nearby was a much older boat, a patched-up bateau of the late 18th century, still bearing traces of jaunty red paint. There was a big iron-hulled passenger boat and another bateau. Scattered around them lay lost belongings and discards of the middle 19th century: a parasol, clay pipes, shoes, bricks, bottles, bits of pottery and china. There was more. A wooden street bridge from the 18th century, pegged together with hardwood trunnels, predated the canal system. It spanned a ravine when Conestoga wagons rumbled through the rude streets of Revolutionary-era Richmond. The bridge had been hidden from view since 1800, when the Great Basin was filled.

In all, recalls one of the dig leaders today, some 60 boats were found and at least partially studied. "But there may have been as many as 200," adds Dr. William E. Trout III. "They were stacked on top of each other." There was plenty of room for such an amazing treasure: the basin, over 40 feet deep in places, was probably the deepest in the United States. As far as canal boats were concerned, the dig was Troy and Pompeii combined. But much was lost.

Today, on the tailored grounds of the James Center, the long-forgotten boatmen who worked the canal, and even the mules that pulled the boats, are memorialized in a handsome bell tower. Inside the new Omni Hotel, floor plaques recall the history underfoot. And the white skyscrapers, like the Dominion Bank Building, that rise from the Great Basin—how do they rate? I read one critical description of the buildings as the kind you see everywhere in the country on the road to the airport, but to me they make a handsome group, by far the best-looking highrise family in town. A satisfying scale and blend of mass and color, a relationship in the windows and walls, establish a unity which the skyline had lacked. The best-looking individual structure as of early 1989, though, may have been Main Street Centre, an elegant taupe-hued highrise several blocks away at Main and Seventh. Meantime the boldest, closest return to the actual riverbank was rising in the twin towers of Riverfront Plaza at 9th and Byrd.

It has been a stately, or perhaps stealthy, process, this refocusing of attention on Richmond's priceless natural asset. Lord knows we have had sufficient time to think about it. As far back as the 1960s the city considered an all-encompassing riverfront redevelopment plan, heavy on recreational facilities and the futuristic development of Belle Isle, but nothing came of it. Now we seem to be creeping back to the bank, and perhaps to the verge of something splendid. The self-guided Canal Walk, a fascinating tour through time that traces historic locks and waterways of exquisite stonework, also takes the walker down to the river itself. I was amazed by the amount of clear, pristine territory there above the tawny boulders lining our river. The site is ripe for sensitive upscale development. What a setting for a residential community of medium highrises! Right in the heart of town, between the lights of the city and the falls of the James! Yet in 1988, when I mentioned the idea to two different developers with the requisite capabilities, each responded negatively. "Richmond isn't ready," one said soberly, as though dipping into a private font of civic wisdom.

He could be right, but Richmond looks ready to me. If we lack one element to become a true renaissance city, it is the presence of a strong, prosperous residential community downtown. We may be getting there by degrees: the upper-story restorations of various early commercial buildings seem to be advancing. But the first builder to erect a stunning 20-story condominium colony within earshot of the falls of the James is the one whose name will be carved on the honored list of true Richmond pioneers and innovators. What a rare, priceless opportunity! It could signal a return to architectural greatness, the days when Jefferson, Robert Mills, and Thomas U. Walter set the standards, backed by citizens who saw no reason why Richmond's standards should be second-rate, leaders with the character, taste, and power to impose mighty works on a community and have them turn out generally right.

It delights me to introduce Richmond to visitors from out of town. The process often begins at the airport, no longer a source of lame jokes and embarrassment. I only wish the authorities hadn't dropped the well-loved, meaningful name, Byrd Field, in the shift to Richmond International Airport. Honoring a Virginian who became a great aviation pioneer, Richard E. Byrd, was the sort of tradition worth retaining. But the facilities themselves, including the new approach road, are huge improvements. The I-64 gateway to town from Byrd Field (forgive me, but old habits die hard) is also the one that greets Tidewater visitors; they are so overcome by the spectacle that for years they have called Richmond The Holy City.

The eastern portal, while not as esthetically gratifying as the southside entrance, is an equally good symbol of modern Richmond. It flashes instant images of activity and the human condition. The blocky stacked enigma of the new Medical College of Virginia Hospital (part of the MCV campus of Virginia Commonwealth University) suggests life, death, and stages in between. The still-splendid bronze mushroom of the Coliseum radiates an aura of circuses, rock concerts, and basketball games. Government workers crowd the sidewalks at midday, reminding the rest of us of the economic virtues of being state capital, and state financial hub.

Any visitor absent since, say, the 1950s would be bewildered by the choice of restaurants, and by the menu of entertainment: theater, concerts, club music, comedy. We have conventions and exhibitions at Richmond Centre. We enjoy the world's musical headliners in that idiosyncratic wonder, the Mosque, and in the Carpenter Center for the Performing Arts, an incomparable movie palace fantasy from the 1920s. There's always something going on, like Arts in the Park, an early spring assembly of artists and craftsmen of generally high skills, spread over Byrd Park on a stupefying scale. An equally Brobdingnagian downtown festival, June Jubilee, is more for music, food, and general whoopee. The Richmond International Music Festival, brightening the air for some two weeks, is a still newer tradition. Such a calendar of festivals has taken up the slack caused when the Tobacco Festival was snuffed out. We can take our children to see the animals at Maymont Park. We can even take dinner

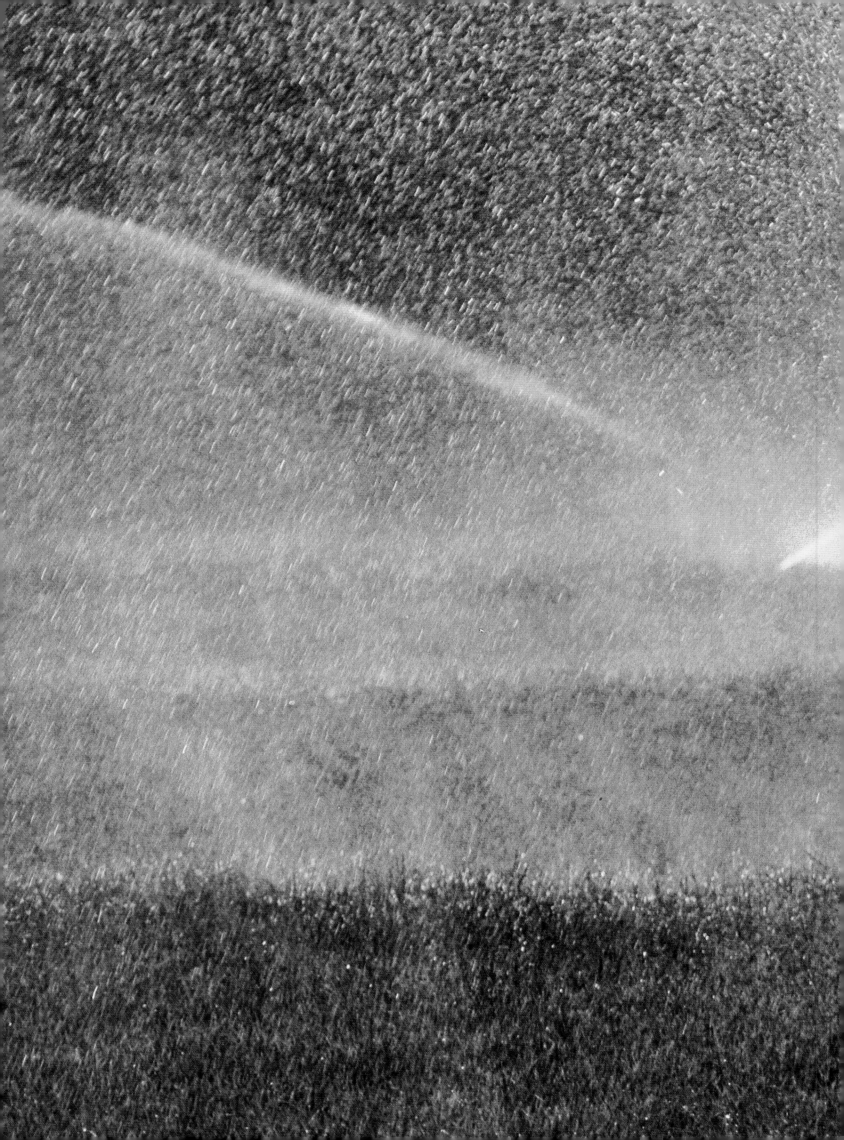

cruises on the James.

It's very nice to fling such assets before visitors to Richmond, but still, the part I enjoy most about having house guests is showing off the traditional city, the unique mixture of memorable history, intriguing buildings, and distinctive neighborhoods. So we load our company in the car and roll, always to the Capitol first. Everyone loves the Capitol. They are amazed to learn that Jefferson played a part in designing it; the very model he sent over from France is still here, and they can see that, too. I remember one friend commenting on the breathtaking audacity of it all, of adopting an exquisite first century Roman temple, La Maison Carrée, for the capitol of a struggling frontier state.

Invariably our visitors are dazzled by the Capitol Rotunda, with its alcove statues of the Virginia-born presidents, circling Houdon's done-from-life marble statue of George Washington standing as it has since 1792, when GW himself came down to approve the placement. It is a work of genius, capturing the colossal strength and character of the man. From the Rotunda we move to the old Hall of the House of Delegates, past the bronze statue of Robert E. Lee, standing on the spot where he cast his lot with the Confederacy. The Capitol guides, in 100-proof Virginia accents, relate their Capitol tales about the trial of Aaron Burr, the Confederate Congress, the history of the Speaker's Chair, and the ghastly collapse of two floors in 1870, killing more than 60 men. Walking through Capitol Square we introduce our guests to some of the Virginians we have honored with statues, like Thomas Jefferson, Patrick Henry, Andrew Lewis, George Mason, John Marshall, Stonewall Jackson, Edgar Allan Poe, and Harry Byrd.

Then we drive through the cobbled streets of Church Hill, haranguing our backseat passengers with tales of the indefatigable Yankee spy Elizabeth Van Lew (whose house, after she died in 1900, still reviled and despised, was expunged by the city like an obnoxious stain), and of Poe's farewell call on his last lady love, Elmira Shelton, whose house has survived. We may visit St. John's Church, where in the yard we point out the grave of Poe's mother. And certainly we recount the story of Patrick Henry's mighty blast of hyperbole, the Liberty or Death speech, delivered right there in that simple clapboard structure. It was already more than 30 years old when Henry electrified the Virginia Convention of 1775.

In Jackson Ward we talk about Maggie Walker, the extraordinary

Preceding pages: Summer children • Randolph Community Center

businesswoman who faced down the double-barreled handicap of being black and female in the heyday of Jim Crow. Her house is now a landmark of the National Park Service. We move on to The Fan, and enjoy hearing our guests marvel at the size and completeness of that enormous turn-of-the-century neighborhood which Richmond somehow preserved intact, a 1900 cityscape now reaching toward 2000 as vital as ever, a place of ferment, a barometer of urban taste, a center of education with the huge academic campus of Virginia Commonwealth University. The Fan embraces a stretch of Monument Avenue, which in certain blocks is a Virginia residential Valhalla. If our visitors' tastes run to serious house viewing, we show them Cary Street Road and assorted side streets, where the spirit of old Richmond seems to hover around stately homes like the sachet of a fresh Bal du Bois corsage. Since the 1920s Richmond's residential taste has run to colonial revival styles, and the pastel-hued look of 18th century Williamsburg is at its best in Richmond's most expensive neighborhoods. (It is a paradox, as the original colonial look was dead by the time Richmond really got going early in the 19th century. The authentic great homes of Richmond began with the federal style, splurged for decades with Greek and Roman revivals, and flirted seriously with Italianate and Gothic reincarnations in the full bloom of Victorian ardor. The only original Georgian-style home in Richmond, Wilton, was moved to Windsor Farms in the 1930s from 15 miles downriver.)

Thenceforward the route of our tour depends entirely on the inclination of our guests. We may look in on the University of Richmond, a picturebook campus, academe incarnate. We may visit the spectral woods of Cold Harbor, most haunted of the region's Civil War battlefields, or drift down through bourbon-tinted swamps to Charles City County, that strangely preserved fragment of the 18th century, and the incomparable plantation trio of Berkeley, Shirley, and Westover. The city cannot be understood without knowing something of what encircles it.

We will certainly show guests at least one, but probably two or three, of Richmond's museums. Is there another city of this size with comparable strength? Even the highly specialized Virginia Historical Society and the still-developing Science Museum of Virginia captivate visitors. And where is there anything like the Edgar Allan Poe Museum? The spirit of Richmond's troubled genius, like the maelstrom of one of Poe's own tales, seems to swirl around the melancholy complex of buildings in Shockoe

Bottom. What a haunted place, there among the inventory of a star-crossed life: his jaunty walking stick; the ravaged mirror of his child bride, Virginia; the parlor furniture from the local mansion of his childhood. A distinctive bird is carved into a dining room chair familiar to the youthful Poe, and you'll never convince me it's not a raven.

All tastes considered, though, the authoritative guest pleaser in Richmond's museum galaxy is the Virginia Museum of Fine Arts. It is our lodestar of artistic culture, and I like the way the Boulevard and Grove giant dazzles first-timers. Thirty-some years ago it was already a good museum, making up in flair what it lacked in gallery space and collections. My wife liked its collection of Fabergé jewelry, one of the world's best, and I always enjoyed the Egyptian collection, where a mummy named Theby rested melodramatically in the dim, dusty reaches of a reconstructed tomb. Today the museum is a different place, four times larger and light years better in its collections. The Fabergé trinkets, those cosmic czarist kickshaws, have retained their popularity, but I prefer to spend my time among the American paintings and furniture, the French impressionists, and the uninhibited delights of the Sydney and Frances Lewis Collection of modern art. The artistic and financial contributions of the Richmond-based Lewises, and of Upperville's Paul Mellon, have been major factors in the progress of this great institution. My only regret about the Virginia Museum of Fine Arts is that somehow along the way, Theby the old Egyptian disappeared. Mummies can't ever seem to rest in peace.

After the Virginia Museum's world view of great art, I like shifting focus to the Valentine Museum's inner scrutiny of Richmond. Sparks fly these days in the block-long row of 19th century houses in the city's ancient "Court End" neighborhood. The Valentine is Richmond's own museum; it is about who we are and how we have behaved. Fast-paced, sometimes controversial, the museum in recent times has tended toward thought-provoking special exhibitions like "In Bondage and Freedom: Antebellum Black Life in Richmond." In early 1989, the Valentine was completing its restoration of the sumptuous 1812 Wickham-Valentine House, one of the city's supreme period mansions. Part of the process was restoring rare neoclassical wall paintings, obliterated since the early Victorian age.

When I rummage in memory through Richmond's museums, I find that none has changed more than the Museum of the Confederacy. In the 1950s, the interior of Jefferson Davis's White House was a warren of oak-

Flag gatherer • reenactment, Hollywood Cemetery

bound display cases, crammed with the raveled leftovers of The Lost
Cause. Labels penned in spidery Spencerian hands described each bullet-
pierced battle flag, each bloodstained butternut jacket, each lock of hair
from some fallen hero's head. In those silent, shadowy, emotion-charged
rooms, you could hear—believe me, you could hear—the faint spine-
chilling echoes of Rebel yells and "Dixie." The establishment was run by
Miss India Thomas, a marvelous personality at once steely and kind,
dedicated and humorous, peppery and gentle. In the early 1960s I asked
her if she ever contemplated changing the displays, which had been set up
in the 1890s. The trend in historical museums was clearly toward more
interpretation and less clutter. I tried to phrase it diplomatically, but Miss
Thomas knew what I meant. She impaled me with a glittering stare.

"This is a memorial," she said. "That is the way to interpret it."

Today's Museum of the Confederacy, set beside the old White House in
a modern building, seems as strong to me—in a contemporary way—as
the old version was as a memorial. The treasure of relics is still
overwhelming, but now you can see and understand them. And the White

House itself! As if Jefferson Davis and his striking lady, the sloe-eyed Varina, had never exited, the house after years of scholarly and expensive restoration has reverted to its 1861–65 state, with authentic, explosively colorful fabrics, wallpaper, rugs, and a great load of original furniture, all correctly in place for the first time in 125 years.

Richmond's role in history as Confederate capital does not seem to put any significant contemporary strain on the city's race relations. The war has come to resemble a mosquito in amber, an exotic, fascinating, but now-stingless relic of eons past. Perhaps the matter turns on a single economic fact: the importance of Civil War history to the city's tourist business. The Late Unpleasantness has an apparently endless world-wide allure. It is the saga with everything, our national historical drama. The late historian Bruce Catton said it was so "mad and overpowering," so melodramatic, as to seem almost unbelievable today. Yet it happened, and a huge part of it happened right in and around our town. But the old, old war is no longer divisive. It's been a long time since I heard anyone accuse Richmonders, or Virginians, of still fighting the Civil War. We don't fight it. The tourists fight it, with cameras, maps, and credit cards. And despite some racial politics, Richmond's bone-deep tradition of civility seems likely to prevail in our relations among ourselves.

When I moved to Richmond I was warned about a certain native reticence. Having come from a Virginia city fully as traditional as Richmond, I knew what to expect in the way of ingrown ancient reserve. It was more of a satisfaction with familiar things and people, and a shyness at being disturbed. In fact I always found Richmonders hospitable in a formal, almost oriental sense. Within their familiar circle was a certain liberal tolerance of eccentricity as long as the eccentric was well-mannered. It is true that, for Richmonders and most other Virginians, time has a different meaning. We sense the presence of our predecessors, and the soft future outlines of our great-grandchildren.

Through all the years I worked for a regular salary, chained to inexorable routine, my wife and I played a little game. We fantasized about where we would live if we were free of our fixed daily agenda and all the imperatives of raising and educating our children. Back to our well-loved home towns? No, you truly cannot go home again. But we enjoyed travel, and as the years passed we would visit new places and then return home to indulge in fresh fantasies. We debated perfect locales and lifestyles. We decided to live in Devon or Yorkshire. No, in France: Paris or Burgundy, definitely. But Highland County, Virginia, might be perfect, we said, or how about the Andalusian coast? The Turkish Aegean? Williamsburg? Costa Rica?

A day came when we awakened with a start and realized we could do it. I was self-employed and could work wherever I plugged in my word processor, and a teacher as good as my wife could always find a position.

The time had come.

We could move anywhere.

And there was no place we wanted to go.

Richmond had snared us, presumably forever, and now each time a new Richmond-born grandchild arrives, I think of Stephen Vincent Benét's lines about our city:

The trees in the streets are old trees used to living with people,
Family trees that remember your grandfather's name.

A town of such character, defining itself in beauty and heritage known nowhere else, becomes a photographer's visual feast. It is also an exacting challenge, heightened by Richmond's infinite variety of subjects. The familiarity of some settings, the subtlety of others, the need to find telling details, juxtapositions, and ironies: such are the demands that David R. White has answered masterfully in the accompanying images.

I especially like the views from overhead. There is something omniscient about close-range aerial photography that recalls a ride I made in the WRVA traffic helicopter. Wafting unobstructed under the flashing blades is so different from fixed-wing flight, which (no matter how small the airplane) glides in its locked linear passage somehow remote from the earth. The copter makes you one with Peter Pan, a spirit swirling through the city's very breath, imbued with a thrilling sense of personal flight. It is magical. You float just over the geometric planes of rooftops on Greek revival houses, the toylike statues of Monument Avenue and Capitol Square, the interstate highways curling liquidly along the routes of forgotten colonial trails, the living silver of our great river, the bright towers by the falls, the tombstones of Hollywood Cemetery sparkling like tossed gravel in the sun. Seen down there, set in a green sea of trees stretching from the Tidewater to the Blue Ridge, Richmond comes together collected and serene, lovable in ancient scars, the tribal hearthstone, The Holy City, our kind of town.

Detail • First National Bank Building

Preceding pages: Aerial • Richmond, viewing east

Architectural detail • Second Presbyterian Church and Main Street Centre

Fountain elms and townhouses • The Fan District

British stone lion • Virginia House entrance way

Byrd Park vita course

Church Hill youths • Chimborazo Playground

Tulips • Bloemendaal

Residence • Jackson Ward

Lunchtime • the financial district

Opposite: Soldiers and Sailors Monument • Libby Hill

Preceding pages: Fog and James River • Goochland County

Sergeant Santa with friends

Young marchers • Richmond Jaycees Christmas Parade

Allegorical figure • equestrian statue of George Washington

James River and bridges • viewing west

Pas de deux, The Nutcracker • *The Concert Ballet*

Opening night • Richmond International Festival of Music

Fall foliage • The Fan District

Preceding pages: Portico • State Capitol

Child and leaves • The Fan District

Neon • Cary Court

Downtown • Dusk

Innsbrook Corporate Center

Architectural detail • The Byrd Theatre

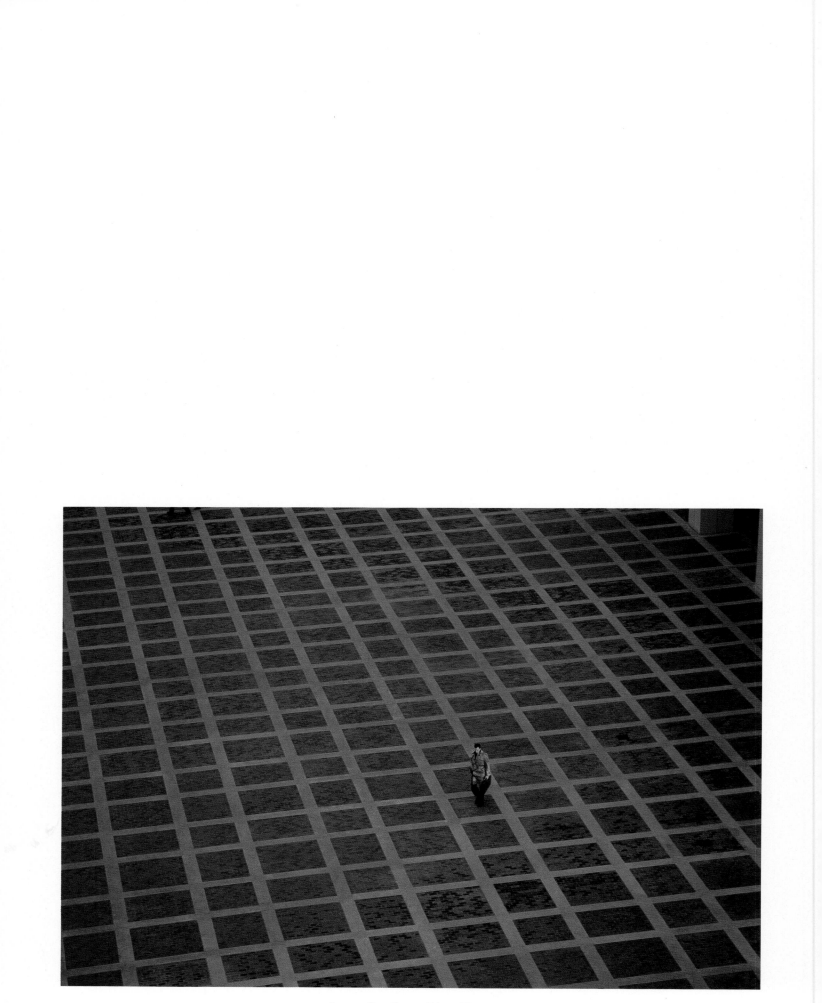

5 pm • One James River Plaza

Northside • Brookland Park

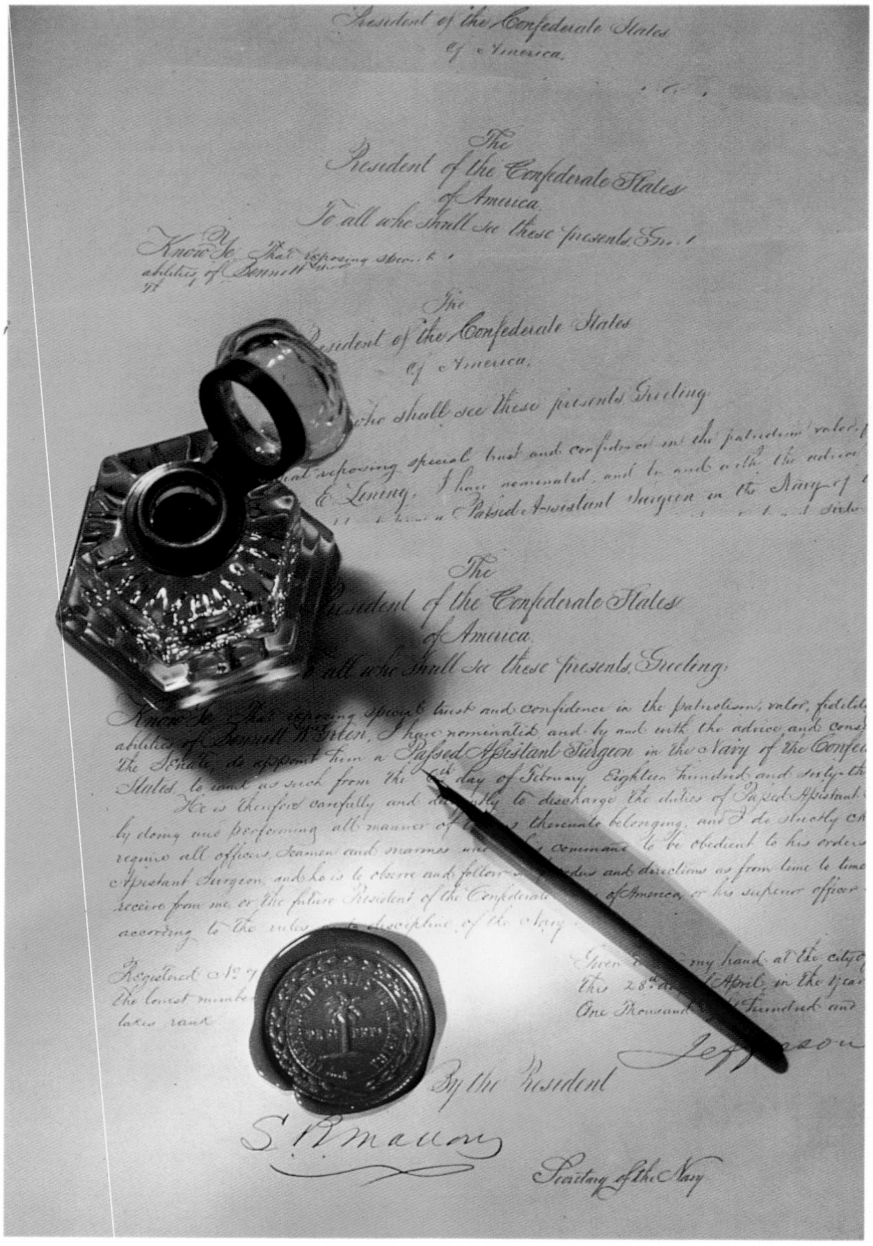

Personal papers • Jefferson Davis

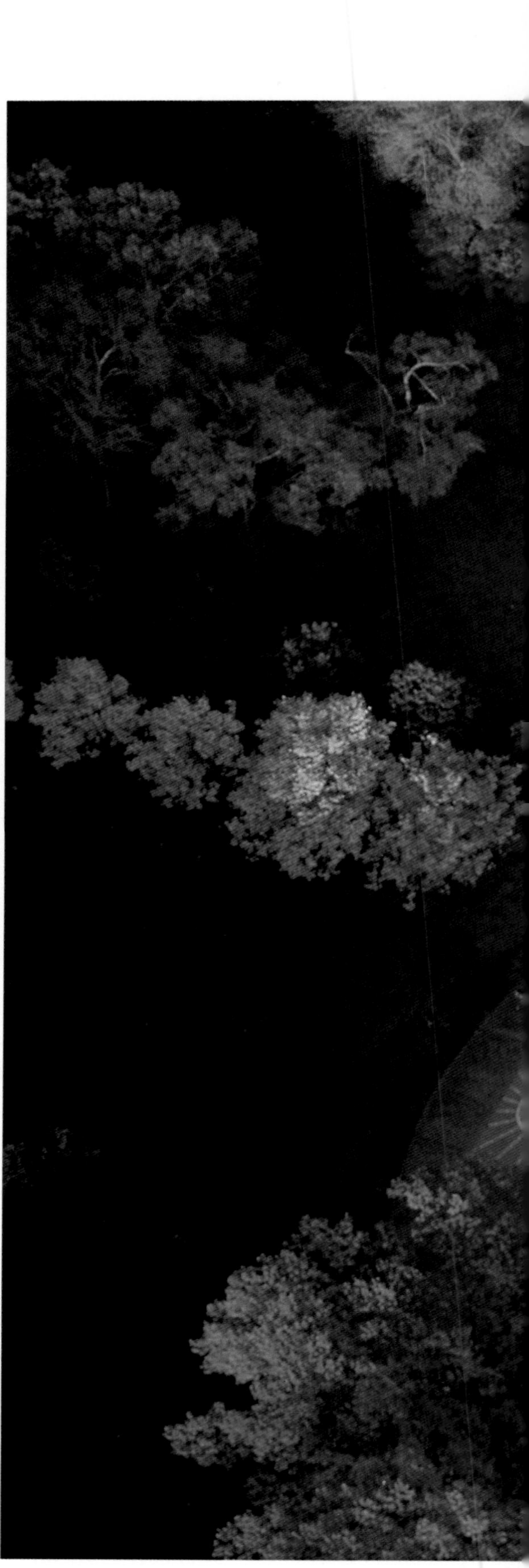

The Carillon • Byrd Park

Graduation Day • Medical College of Virginia, Virginia Commonwealth University

Preceding pages: Confederate Memorial Day

Miss Gold Bowl • Gold Bowl Classic, Hovey Field, Virginia Union University

Morning workout • Jefferson Hill Park

Memory • *The Virginia War Memorial*

Railroad yard • near west end

Industrial southside and downtown

Dancer • Patriotism Day

Preceding pages: Monument Avenue

72

Volleyball players • Innsbrook Corporate Center

Sculptor's studio • The Valentine Museum

Governor's portrait gallery • State Capitol

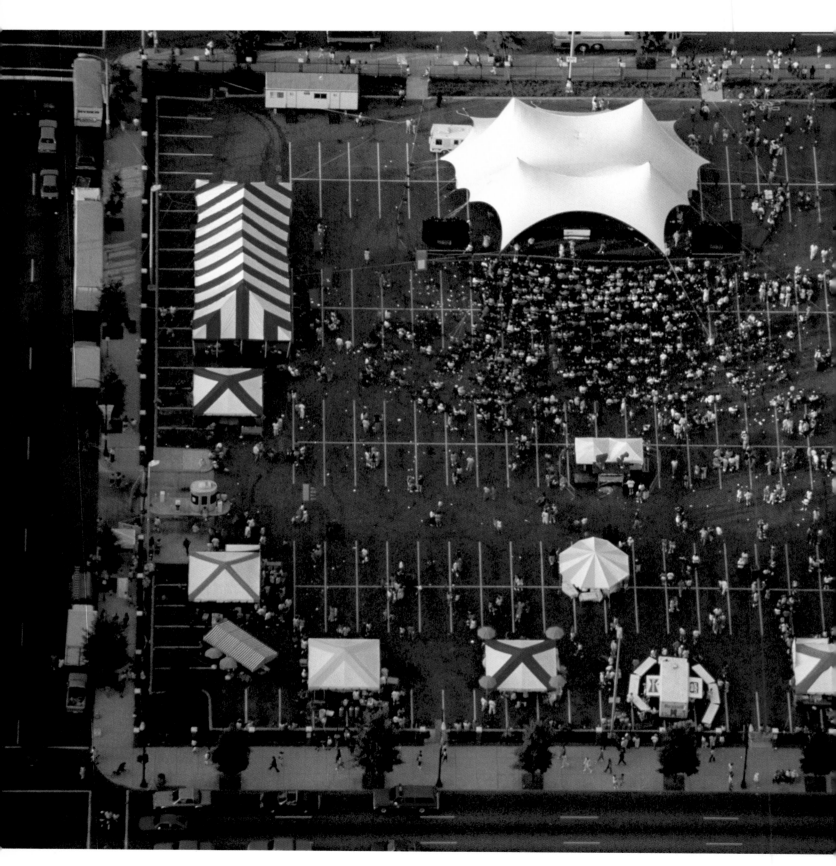

Tents • June Jubilee

Mother and son • Kanawha Plaza

Maggie L. Walker House • Jackson Ward

Ironwork and townhouses • The Fan District

Skier in Shockoe Slip

Preceding pages: Spring plowing • Hanover County

November snow • The Virginia State Capitol

Glass and reflections • The Branch House

Victorian Day • Maymont Park

Wheel chair competitors • The Richmond Marathon

Members, Colonel's Company • First Virginia Regiment

Springtime • Monument Avenue

Stretches • The Richmond Marathon

The University of Richmond

The Dooley Mansion • Maymont Park

Medical College of Virginia, Virginia Commonwealth University

Preceding pages: Fishermen • James River

Horseman • Strawberry Hill Races

Saint John's Church • Church Hill

Church Hill • viewing east

Christmas Luminaries • Chesterfield County

Illuminated reindeer display • James Center

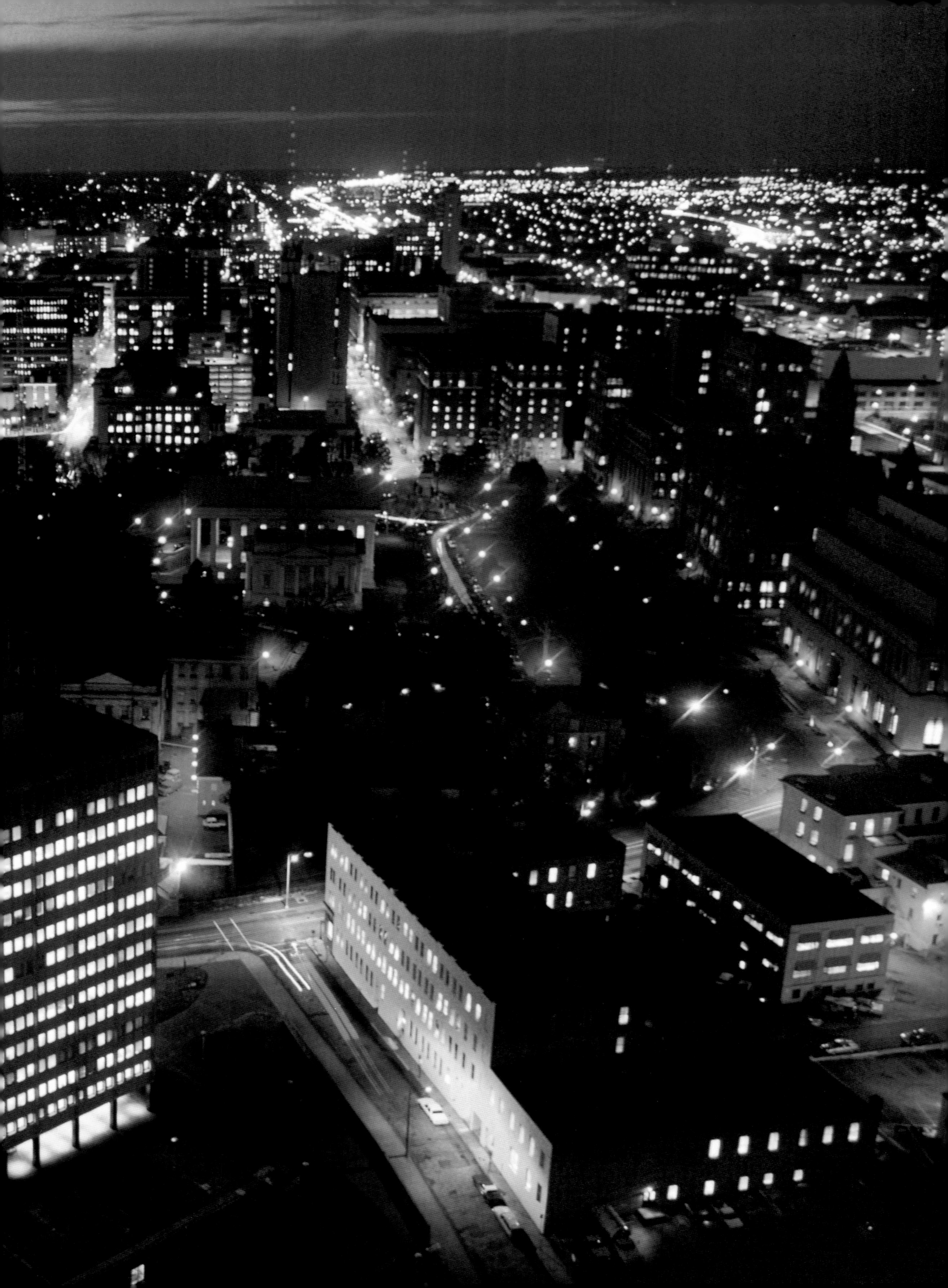

Participant • Richmond International Festival of Music

Preceding pages: Downtown • viewing west

West Wing • Virginia Museum of Fine Arts

State Fair of Virginia

Sledding and sliding • Forest Hill Park

Mounted policeman • Richmond Children's Festival

Opposite: Musket volley • 200th anniversary of Virginia's signing of the Constitution.

Dawn • Richmond and the James River

Monument in fog • Robert E. Lee

109

Plaza • The James Monroe Building

Opposite: Science Museum of Virginia

Parlor view • Agecroft Hall

Preceding pages: Rooftops • Monument Avenue

Soldier with ponytail • Patriotism Day

Dancers at intermission, The Nutcracker • *The Richmond Ballet*

Little Dancer Fourteen Years Old, *Edgar Degas;* Mother and Child,
*Rober Bouguereau. French Collection, Late 18th and 19th Century
Virginia Museum of Fine Arts*

Main Street Station and Interstate 95

Opposite: Pyramid • Hollywood Cemetery

Preceding pages: Shirley Plantation

The Three Graces • *Maymont Park*

Monument • J. E. B. Stuart

Following pages: Balloonists • Hanover County

PICTORIAL NOTES

prepared by David R. White

1   A gas street lamp, one of many located in the city's historic districts, glows at dusk among the petals of a pink dogwood.

2–3   This statue of Hunter Holmes McGuire, M.D., LL. D. (1835–1900), founder of the University College of Medicine, is located on the north side of the Virginia State Capitol.

4–5   A heavy February snowfall provides a couple with a tranquil afternoon in Forest Hill Park.

6–7   James Center Complex in the Shockoe Bottom area of the city, viewing east.

10   This statue to Maury, "Pathfinder of the Seas" and Commodore of the Confederate Navy, is located at Belmont Street and Monument Avenue.

14–15   A materials barge and tugboat heading toward the city pass the Port of Richmond, located on the James River, on the southside. Formerly named Deepwater Terminal, the Port of Richmond is the westernmost port on the North Atlantic.

18   See text, pages 18–19.

22–23   A group of youngsters enjoys the refreshing mist of the sprinkling system for the Randolph Community Center playing field.

26–27   A participant in the annual Confederate Day Heritage Parade gathers miniature Confederate flags in Hollywood Cemetery.

30–31   Made from an elevation of 800 feet, this expansive view shows the Kanawha Canal, which parallels the James River's north bank and is adjacent to Hollywood Cemetery.

33   A column capital and bas-relief panels are shown in this detail view of the First National Bank Building in the heart of the city's financial district.

33   An architectural detail of the 19th-century Second Presbyterian Church in contrast to the recently completed Main Street Centre.

34–35   Morning light outlines these townhouses and fountain elms on Hanover Avenue.

35   A British stone lion greets visitors at the entranceway of Virginia House, located in Windsor Farms.

36   Afternoon joggers finish the one-mile Vita Course in Byrd Park.

36–37   Almost parallel to the ground, children propel themselves skyward on a bright July morning.

38–39   Bloemendaal Farm, located at Lewis Ginter Botanical Gardens on the northside, vividly portrays the beauty of spring.

39   A Jackson Ward residence proudly displays the renovation efforts of private owners.

40–41   Viewing east at 800 feet, 6:45 am, April 1989, west of Richmond over Goochland County.

42   On one of the first warm days of spring in the financial district of Main Street, lunch becomes an outside occasion.

43   Dedicated in 1894, the Soldiers and Sailors Monument stands high atop Libby Hill Park in historic Church Hill.

44   Richmond's own "Sergeant Santa": Sergeant Ricky Duling, Richmond Police Department (retired, 1989). The Sergeant Santa program began in 1972 as a way to encourage children to trust rather than feel intimidated by a police officer. It has been so successful that, even though retired, Duling will continue his work year-round. A special thank you to Ricky Duling.

45   These young ladies are just moments away from the start of the annual Richmond Jaycees Christmas Parade.

46   One of six allegorical figures at the base of the equestrian statue of George Washington on the grounds of the State Capitol.

46–47   The James River railroad bridge and Powhite Parkway bridge, viewing west.

48   The Concert Ballet, a civic company, performs in Richmond and throughout the state in full-scale touring programs.

48–49   The United Nations Singers opened the first annual city-wide festival of music, which drew more than 20,000 to Fountain Lake in Byrd Park in 1988.

50–51   A jet airliner's lights create a streak on the film during a 20-second time exposure. The plane is departing Richmond International Airport 12 miles to the east.

52–53   The green leaves of a yet-unturned sycamore tree provide a contrast to the silver maple in the background, which has almost reached its peak of color transformation.

53   A young Fan District toddler takes a break from the pleasant task of sweeping leaves on a crisp fall morning.

54–55   An expansive view of downtown Richmond, looking west.

56–57   The changing face of Richmond's contemporary architecture is shown here in this reflective detail of the Markel Building, located in western Henrico County.

57   This elegantly crafted detail of historic Byrd Theater in Carytown gleams in the late afternoon light.

60   Still life of Jefferson Davis's desk in the recently restored White House of the Confederacy.

60–61   The Carillon, seen from 800 feet. A memorial to those who died in World War I, the Carillon is located in Byrd Park near the amphitheater of Dogwood Dell.

62–63   On a hot and humid May day, participants in the annual Confederate Memorial Day Heritage Parade enjoy a refreshing spring shower during a moment of prayer.

64–65   Their next step a medical residency, these newly conferred doctors accept their diplomas at June commencement. Combined enrollments of both MCV and VCU's West Campus exceed 21,000.

65   Newly elected queen at the annual Gold Bowl Classic of Virginia Union University. The pageant encourages participation of young persons in a collegiate activity. The queen and her two attendants are each awarded scholarships.

66–67   Viewing west from Jefferson Hill Park at 21st and East Marshall Streets. A runner begins his early morning workout while the city awakens in the background.

67   Located just north of the Lee Bridge, the Virginia War Memorial honors those from the Commonwealth who died in World War II, Korea, and Vietnam. A statue, "Memory," and an eternal flame, "The Torch of Liberty," honor those whose names are etched in an expansive glass wall.

68   The Richmond Fredericksburg and Potomac Railroad's ACCA yard, viewed from 1000 feet, is more than two miles long. The facility handles more than 28,000 cars per month.

69   Factories, warehouses, and manufacturing outlets punctuate the landscape in this view from 1200 feet of industrial southside. To the north, the buildings of downtown Richmond reflect the afternoon light.

70–71   Traffic flows east and west on Monument Avenue under a full October moon.

72   A dancer gives a high kick and a smart salute during the annual Patriotism Day performance at the Carillon in Byrd Park.

73   Competitors leap, swat and smash in an after-5pm volleyball game at Innsbrook in western Henrico County.

74   Civil War figures cast an enigmatic glow in the studio of Edward V. Valentine, noted sculptor during that period.

75   Surrounding the entire third floor of the State Capitol, these commissioned paintings portray those who have held Virginia's most distinguished office.

76–77   A parking lot in downtown Richmond becomes a festive tent-city for the annual June Jubilee Celebration of the Arts.

77   A mother and son enjoy the cool spray of a cascading waterfall at Kanawha Plaza just south of the James Center Complex.

78–79 In this front parlor of the Maggie L. Walker National Historic Site hangs a photograph of one of America's most prominent black female leaders in business and civic affairs. Below the image is the wheelchair to which she was confined for more than 20 years until her death at age 67 (1934). Located in historic Jackson Ward, her home is less than three blocks east of a special monument to another prominent Richmond citizen, William "Bojangles" Robinson.

79 Along Stuart Avenue in the Fan District, colorful townhouses and their unique ornamental ironwork.

82 Historic Shockoe Slip was transformed into a two-cityblock, man-made ski slope for Wintergreen-Winterfest 1989. The event was funded by area businesses to benefit the Special Olympics program.

83 With the portico of Virginia's State Capitol in the background, a solitary figure walks along the capitol grounds during a surprise November snowstorm.

84 Designed by John Russell Pope and modeled after the Compton-Wynate Mansion in England, the Branch House was constructed in 1918 as a private residence. Pope was also the architect for such treasures as the Jefferson Memorial, the National Gallery, and Broad Street Station (Richmond).

84–85 A Richmond couple with proper furry companion relaxes after the carriage parade at Victorian Day in Maymont Park. Held each fall, the event features carriage rides and high wheel cyclists in vintage costumes.

86 Leading the way for more than 3,000 entrants, these athletes start the race for the Richmond Marathon. Sponsored by Richmond Newspapers and first held in 1978, the 26.2-mile race draws competitors from around the world. The event, held each October, starts and finishes in Shockoe Slip.

87 Dressed as soldiers in Revolutionary War uniforms, these two are actually full-time members of the United States Army.

88 This aerial view of Monument Avenue and its beautiful median strip shows the statues of Robert E. Lee (bottom) and J.E.B. Stuart.

89 Preparing to go the distance, this runner "stretches out" in the staging area for the Richmond Marathon.

90–91 Located in the far west end, this early morning aerial view shows the campuses of Westhampton College and Richmond College. Together with the T.C. Williams Law School, they comprise the University of Richmond, the largest independent university in Virginia.

91 The opulent Dooley Mansion, former home of Confederate veteran Major James H. Dooley, is a Victorian extravaganza. Both the mansion and its 105 acres were donated to the city, creating Maymont Park.

92–93 A summer fisherman casts a line just west of Richmond's "Nickel Bridge" into the tepid waters of the James River. Further east on the James and into its outlying tributaries was held the renowned BASS Masters Tournament in the summers of 1988 and 1989.

94 Donated to the Medical College of Virginia in 1985, this statue of Hippocrates with its prophetic inscription was a gift from Virginians of Greek Ancestry.

95 An annual rite of spring, the Strawberry Hill Races are complete with strawberries and cream and a carriage parade through the city.

96 In 1775 at the Virginia Convention, Patrick Henry proclaimed the immortal words, "Give me liberty or give me death," at St. John's Church, then the largest meeting place in Richmond.

98–99 In the subdivision of Surreywood and its surrounding neighborhoods in Chesterfield County, residents proudly display thousands of lights commencing on Christmas Eve.

99 For more than a 15-day period in December and early January, the James Center Complex is transformed into a fantasyland of illuminated trees and magic reindeer.

102 A member of the United Nations Staff Recreation Council Singers rehearses near Byrd's Fountain Lake.

103 This new 90,000 square foot addition to the Virginia Museum establishes the museum as the largest in the Southeast.

104–5 Held each September at the Virginia State Fairgrounds, the State Fair highlights Virginia's largest industry—agriculture.

105 A guarantee with every appreciable snowfall is the tradition of sledding at Forest Hill Park on the city's southside.

106 One of six mounted policemen of the Richmond Police Department, this officer and his gentle mount are an attractive curiosity for youths and children at the Richmond Children's Festival.

107 Participants in the 200th anniversary of Virginia's signing of the Constitution fire a volley salute in celebration of the event.

108–9 Sunrise at 800 feet, October 1987, two miles west of Richmond.

109 This statue depicting General Robert E. Lee astride his famous horse Traveller is at the intersection of Monument and Allen Avenues.

110 A youngster eager to explore and discover creates a complete reflection of himself at the Science Museum of Virginia. The giant "pods" are actually the outer walls of "Crystal World," a massive hands-on exhibit in the lobby of the museum.

111 In operation 24 hours a day for the State of Virginia, the 25-story James Monroe Building, one of the city's tallest structures, is located at 14th and East Franklin Streets.

114–15 This Tudor manor house constructed in England (15th century) was moved to Richmond in the 1920's. In this sundown view of a corner of the Great Parlor is a volume of essays by James I and an intricately crafted English "turned" chair (circa 1640).

116–17 Started as a civic company in 1963, the Richmond Ballet moved to professional status in 1984. With a growing national reputation the distinguished company provides an excellent environment for training in dance and attracts dancers from across the United States. The company also operates the School of the Richmond Ballet, with programs, classes and workshops throughout the year. Its annual performance of *The Nutcracker* at the Mosque is a highlight of the Christmas season.

117 Purchased in 1945 by the Museum, this Degas sculpture is one of 27 throughout the world. The wax model of the cast work was the only sculpture he exhibited in his lifetime.

118–19 Located only 18 miles east of Richmond on historic Route 5, Shirley Plantation was founded in 1614 and eventually registered in 1660 by Edward Hill, ancestor of Charles Hill Carter, the present owner.

120 Located on East Main Street just west of the city's 17th Street Farmer's Market, Main Street Station was erected in 1901 by the Seaboard Air Line Railway C&O Railroad.

121 This 90-foot pyramid is a monument to the more than 18,000 Confederate soldiers buried in Hollywood Cemetery. Established in 1849 as the city's first private cemetery, it is also the burial place for Jefferson Davis, James Monroe, J.E.B. Stuart, and John Tyler.

122 A different perspective of the "Three Graces" affords a view of the intricate stone carving indicative of the 1920's.

122–23 This monument to Stuart, erected in 1907, is located at Lombardy Street and Monument Avenue.

124–25 With the city some 12 miles to the east, balloonists project their vessel towards the heavens. This photograph was made at an elevation of 2200 feet.

FINISHED . . .

No one person is ever responsible for the culmination of a creative activity. Numerous individuals, often people simply doing their everyday jobs, provided me with the help and guidance toward the photographic efforts necessary for the completion of this book. So many Richmond citizens were invaluable and totally unselfish with their time, interest, and assistance.

During this extremely demanding period friends and family shared with me more of themselves than I could ever imagine or request. Certain individuals associated with this project either directly or indirectly deserve a special mention for their participation and assistance.

Robert Llewellyn, who has been involved with 15 books of this type continually provided his encouragement and expertise as a friend and photographer. *Jeffrey Burt,* the book's designer, always gave his enthusiasm and energy despite the many changes and revisions associated with publishing. *Hal* and *Reba McVey* shared with me their special cottage in a place known as "Little Richmond" in Gloucester, Virginia, for editing and quiet time. *Jeffrey Allison,* STOCKFILE'S office manager and picture researcher, kept me organized with the more than 6,000 photographs considered for the book. *Ani Lytle,* publication representative, pre-sold this idea to many corporations and businesses in the city, providing us with the financial support needed to go to press. *Jim Wamsley,* author of the text, personified the notion that the "art of writing" was committed rewriting. *Susan Heroy,* editorial assistant, added the objective scrutiny necessary with a project of this magnitude. *Peter Bacque* and *Nancy Jaeger,* pilots at Hanover Aviation, were invaluable in my efforts to produce aerial photographs.

For my wife *Lin* and our son *Jacob,* thank you for the understanding and time to be away from home on too many occasions.

July 9, 1989

David R. White
Photographer